Understanding Cortisol:

The Key to Managing Stress, Boosting Health, and Living a Balanced Life

By Dr. Alexander Montrose

Copyright © 2024 by Dr. Alexander Montrose

All rights reserved. No part of this book may be reproduced, distributed, or transmitted in any form or by any means, including photocopying, recording, or other electronic or mechanical methods, without the prior written permission of the author, except in the case of brief quotations embodied in critical reviews and certain other non-commercial uses permitted by copyright law.

First Edition: 2024

ISBN: 9798344248424

Published by Amazon Kindle Direct Publishing

Printed in the United States of America

Disclaimer: The information provided in this book is intended for general informational purposes only and should not be considered as professional medical advice. Readers are encouraged to consult with their healthcare professional for any specific medical concerns.

Table of Contents

Introduction 4

Chapter 1: What is Cortisol? 6

Chapter 2: What Increases Cortisol Levels? 18

Chapter 3: The Impact of Cortisol on Your Body and Mind 27

Chapter 4: Nutrition and Cortisol: The Power of Food 38

Chapter 5: Exercise and Cortisol: Finding the Right Balance 50

Chapter 6: The Importance of Sleep: Resting Your Way to Hormonal Balance 60

Chapter 7: Stress Management Techniques: Lowering Cortisol Through Mindfulness and Relaxation 71

Chapter 8: Environmental and Lifestyle Adjustments for Lower Cortisol 83

Chapter 9: Creating a Sustainable Low-Cortisol Lifestyle 96

About the Author 110

Dr. Alexander Montrose

Introduction

In our fast-paced modern world, stress has become an unavoidable part of life. Whether it's balancing demanding careers, family obligations, or financial pressures, many of us constantly juggle multiple responsibilities. As a result, our bodies and minds often bear the burden of chronic stress. At the heart of this stress response is a hormone you may have heard of but likely misunderstood—cortisol.

Often dubbed the "stress hormone," cortisol is critical for our survival, helping us respond quickly and effectively to stressors. However, prolonged exposure to elevated cortisol levels can wreak havoc on our health, leading to weight gain, fatigue, anxiety, and even serious conditions like heart disease and diabetes.

This book is your guide to understanding cortisol—what it is, how it works, and how it influences nearly every aspect of your health. More importantly, you'll learn practical strategies to manage cortisol levels effectively. Whether you're struggling with stress, seeking to improve your health, or simply wanting to live a more balanced life, this book will provide the tools and insights you need.

From exploring the science of cortisol to offering actionable tips on nutrition, exercise, sleep, and mindfulness, you'll discover how small changes in your daily routine can help keep cortisol in check and lead to greater well-being. Let's embark on this journey together to regain control over stress, boost your health, and create a more balanced and fulfilling life.

Chapter 1:
What is Cortisol?

Cortisol is a hormone that is often misunderstood and associated only with stress. But it's much more than just a "stress hormone." In reality, cortisol is essential for life. It's involved in regulating many vital processes in the body, such as metabolism, immune response, and even brain function. When balanced, cortisol helps us stay alert and focused, regulate blood sugar levels, manage inflammation, and maintain a healthy energy supply.

However, when cortisol levels are imbalanced—whether too high or too low—it can cause a variety of problems, from anxiety and fatigue to weight gain and chronic illness. In this chapter, we'll dive into the biology of cortisol, exploring what it is, how it works, and why it's crucial to our well-being.

1.1
The Role of Cortisol in the Body

Cortisol is a steroid hormone produced by the adrenal glands, which sit on top of your kidneys. Its production is controlled by the **hypothalamic-pituitary-adrenal (HPA) axis**, a complex feedback system that helps regulate many bodily functions, especially in response to stress.

When your brain perceives a threat, whether it's physical or emotional, the hypothalamus sends a signal to the pituitary gland, which then releases adrenocorticotropic hormone (ACTH). This hormone travels through your bloodstream to your adrenal glands, prompting them to release cortisol. Once cortisol is released into your bloodstream, it prepares your body to deal with the stressor.

Some of cortisol's key functions include:

- **Regulating metabolism:** Cortisol helps convert proteins, fats, and carbohydrates into energy, especially when your body is under stress. This process ensures that your brain and muscles have enough fuel to respond to a stressful situation.

- **Managing blood sugar levels:** Cortisol raises blood sugar by stimulating glucose production in the liver and breaking down muscle tissue to release amino acids. This is why chronic stress, which leads to prolonged cortisol elevation, is associated with higher blood sugar levels and an increased risk of diabetes.

- **Controlling inflammation:** Cortisol is a powerful anti-inflammatory hormone. It suppresses the immune system to prevent excessive inflammation during times of stress. However, when cortisol levels remain high for too long, it can weaken the immune system, making you more vulnerable to infections and illnesses.

- **Supporting memory and cognitive function:** Cortisol influences brain function, particularly in areas like the hippocampus, which is responsible for memory and learning. In small doses, cortisol can improve memory and focus, but chronic high cortisol can impair cognitive function and even shrink the hippocampus over time.

1.2
Cortisol's Evolutionary Role: Survival and Adaptation

Cortisol has played a fundamental role in human evolution, especially in helping early humans survive in hostile environments. As a crucial part of the "fight or flight" response, cortisol helped our ancestors react quickly to physical threats such as predators, environmental dangers, or even rival human groups. The hormone's ability to mobilize energy rapidly, suppress non-essential functions, and focus attention on immediate survival allowed early humans to escape danger or fight when necessary.

The problem we face today, however, is that many of the stressors triggering cortisol are not life-threatening. Instead, we experience psychological stress from daily life—work deadlines, family pressures, financial concerns—that keeps our cortisol levels elevated for prolonged periods. While our ancestors might have faced short bursts of intense stress followed by long recovery periods, modern life often exposes us to **chronic stress**.

The Fight-or-Flight Mechanism

The "fight or flight" mechanism is deeply ingrained in our biology, a result of millions of years of evolution. When faced with a perceived threat, our bodies prepare to either confront the danger or flee from it. The release of cortisol is central to this response, but it is not alone. The **sympathetic nervous system** also plays a role, activating the adrenal glands to release adrenaline and norepinephrine, which increase heart rate and blood flow to muscles.

Here's what happens during a typical "fight or flight" response:

- **Energy surge:** Cortisol increases blood sugar levels by converting stored glycogen into glucose, providing quick energy to the muscles and brain.

- **Increased alertness:** Cortisol sharpens attention and focus, ensuring you are fully aware of the threat and able to react swiftly.

- **Suppression of non-essential functions:** Processes like digestion, reproduction, and immune function are temporarily suppressed, allowing the body to prioritize energy and resources for immediate survival.

In the past, once the threat passed, cortisol levels would return to normal. However, the constant exposure to stress in modern life keeps our bodies in a near-perpetual state of heightened cortisol production, with serious consequences for our health.

The Impact of Modern Stressors on Cortisol

While early humans faced clear, physical stressors, today's stressors are often psychological and much more complex. A constant barrage of emails, social media notifications, job-related pressures, and even financial stress can trigger the same cortisol response as a physical threat, but the release of cortisol is often unnecessary and excessive.

This is where the mismatch between our biology and modern life becomes problematic. Chronic psychological stress keeps cortisol levels elevated long after the original stressor has passed, and over time, this can lead to a range of health problems such as **chronic inflammation**, **weakened immune response**, and **metabolic dysfunction**.

Case Study: The Office Worker's Cortisol Dilemma

Consider John, a 45-year-old office worker. His day starts with an early alarm and a rush to get ready, followed by an hour-long commute through heavy traffic. Once at work, he juggles tight deadlines, frequent meetings, and a constant flow of emails. By the time he leaves the office, he's already feeling mentally and physically exhausted. However, the stress doesn't end there—John's cortisol levels remain elevated well into the evening as he worries about the next day's tasks, his finances, and personal obligations.

Like many modern workers, John is living in a state of **chronic stress**. His body is constantly producing cortisol to cope with these demands, leading to sleep problems, weight gain, and a growing sense of fatigue. Over time, this pattern of elevated cortisol could contribute to the development of more serious conditions like heart disease, anxiety disorders, or even Type 2 diabetes.

1.3
The Hypothalamic-Pituitary-Adrenal (HPA) Axis: Cortisol's Control Center

Cortisol is part of a larger system known as the **hypothalamic-pituitary-adrenal (HPA) axis**, a complex communication network between the brain and the adrenal glands that regulates your body's stress response. Understanding how this system works is crucial to managing cortisol levels effectively.

How the HPA Axis Works

The HPA axis is activated whenever the brain perceives a threat or stressor. The process begins with the **hypothalamus**, a small region at the base of the brain responsible for regulating many bodily functions, including hunger, sleep, and stress. When the hypothalamus detects stress, it releases **corticotropin-releasing hormone (CRH)**, which signals the **pituitary gland** (also located in the brain) to release **adrenocorticotropic hormone (ACTH)**. ACTH then travels through the bloodstream to the adrenal glands, prompting them to release cortisol.

Once cortisol levels rise, the body is primed to respond to the stressor. Cortisol's effects are systemic, meaning they influence multiple organs and systems throughout the body. Once the perceived threat is resolved, cortisol levels should decrease, and the HPA axis will return to its normal state. However, in situations of chronic stress, the HPA axis can become dysregulated, leading to continuous cortisol production.

Negative Feedback: Keeping Cortisol in Check

The HPA axis operates on a **negative feedback loop**, meaning that cortisol itself helps regulate its own production. When cortisol levels rise to a certain point, it sends signals back to the hypothalamus and pituitary gland to reduce CRH and ACTH production, thereby slowing cortisol release. This feedback mechanism ensures that cortisol levels don't remain too high for too long.

However, chronic stress can impair this feedback loop. When the body is constantly exposed to stressors, the HPA axis becomes less sensitive to cortisol's regulatory signals. This leads to prolonged periods of elevated cortisol, which can eventually cause the adrenal glands to become overworked, leading to a condition known as **adrenal fatigue**.

1.4
The Critical Functions of Cortisol in the Body

Cortisol's primary role is to help the body manage stress, but its effects are much broader. In this section, we'll explore how cortisol influences several key systems in the body.

Metabolism: Cortisol's Role in Energy Production

One of cortisol's key functions is regulating metabolism. When the body is under stress, cortisol ensures that there's enough glucose in the bloodstream to fuel the brain and muscles. It does this by stimulating **gluconeogenesis**, a process in which the liver converts non-carbohydrate sources like amino acids into glucose.

At the same time, cortisol suppresses the body's insulin response, making it harder for cells to take up glucose from the bloodstream. This ensures that glucose remains available for immediate use by the brain and muscles. However, this process also has a downside: chronically elevated cortisol levels can lead to high blood sugar, insulin resistance, and, eventually, **Type 2 diabetes**.

Practical Tip: Managing Blood Sugar to Control Cortisol

Maintaining stable blood sugar levels is crucial for keeping cortisol in check. Eating balanced meals with a mix of protein, healthy fats, and complex carbohydrates can help prevent blood sugar spikes and crashes, which in turn reduces the need for cortisol to regulate energy.

The Immune System: Cortisol's Anti-Inflammatory Power

Cortisol has a powerful anti-inflammatory effect, which is why synthetic versions of the hormone (such as prednisone) are often prescribed to treat inflammatory conditions like asthma or rheumatoid arthritis. During times of stress, cortisol suppresses the immune system to prevent it from overreacting to perceived threats.

However, prolonged high cortisol levels can weaken the immune system over time, making the body more susceptible to infections. Chronic high cortisol can also contribute to **autoimmune diseases**, where the immune system mistakenly attacks the body's own tissues.

Case Study: Cortisol and Autoimmune Disease

Sarah, a 30-year-old woman with a demanding job, began experiencing chronic fatigue, joint pain, and frequent illnesses. After seeing a doctor, she was diagnosed with **lupus**, an autoimmune disorder. Her doctor explained that chronic stress had likely contributed to her condition by keeping her cortisol levels elevated and weakening her immune system. Through stress management techniques, Sarah was able to reduce her cortisol levels and improve her symptoms.

The Brain: Cortisol's Effect on Memory and Learning

Cortisol's influence on the brain is both beneficial and harmful, depending on how long and how often it is elevated. In the short term, cortisol enhances memory and learning by boosting activity in the **hippocampus**, the part of the brain responsible for processing and storing memories.

However, chronic stress and elevated cortisol levels can damage the hippocampus over time, impairing memory and learning. Research has shown that individuals with high cortisol levels have smaller hippocampal volumes, which is linked to memory problems, cognitive decline, and even an increased risk of **Alzheimer's disease**.

Practical Tip: Protecting Brain Health

One of the best ways to protect your brain from the damaging effects of cortisol is to practice stress-relief techniques like mindfulness and meditation, which have been shown to reduce cortisol levels and improve cognitive function. Regular physical exercise, particularly aerobic exercise, can also help protect the brain from cortisol's negative effects by promoting neurogenesis (the growth of new brain cells) in the hippocampus.

Chapter 2:
What Increases Cortisol Levels?

Understanding what causes cortisol levels to rise is essential in learning how to manage it effectively. Cortisol production is triggered by a variety of factors, ranging from physical stress (such as illness or injury) to psychological stress (such as anxiety, trauma, or chronic worry). In this chapter, we'll explore the main contributors to elevated cortisol and the mechanisms behind them.

2.1
Physical Stressors: The Body's Reaction to Injury, Illness, and Exercise

Cortisol is often thought of as the body's primary stress hormone because it helps mobilize energy and resources to handle physical challenges. But it isn't only psychological stress that increases cortisol—physical stressors such as injury, illness, pain, and even exercise can also cause a surge in cortisol levels.

Injury and Cortisol

When you experience a physical injury—whether it's something as small as a cut or as significant as a broken bone—your body needs to direct resources toward healing. Cortisol plays a major role in this process by suppressing inflammation (which can become excessive) and by providing the energy required for tissue repair.

For example, let's consider the case of **Linda**, a 40-year-old avid cyclist who suffered a major accident during a race, breaking her leg in several places. In the immediate aftermath of the accident, her body responded by releasing cortisol, along with other hormones like adrenaline, to reduce inflammation and begin the healing process. Cortisol helped ensure that her body could prioritize healing while also suppressing pain and discomfort. However, during the long recovery process, Linda's cortisol levels remained elevated for months, contributing to feelings of fatigue, anxiety, and difficulty sleeping.

Linda's experience is not uncommon; many people dealing with physical trauma or illness experience prolonged periods of elevated cortisol. While this can be beneficial for short-term recovery, chronic high cortisol levels can weaken the immune system and prolong healing if left unchecked.

Illness and Cortisol

When your body is fighting off an illness, whether it's a cold, flu, or more serious infection, cortisol levels rise to help manage the immune response. Cortisol temporarily suppresses inflammation and prevents the immune system from overreacting, ensuring that the body's defense mechanisms are balanced.

However, **chronic illness** can cause cortisol levels to remain elevated for long periods. Take the example of **George**, a 55-year-old man with a history of autoimmune diseases like rheumatoid arthritis. For George, his immune system is constantly in a state of hyperactivity, attacking healthy tissues in his body. His body's response is to release more cortisol to manage inflammation, but this long-term elevation in cortisol has led to weight gain, muscle loss, and difficulty regulating his blood sugar.

In cases like George's, managing cortisol becomes a critical part of managing the disease itself. Without proper intervention, his body is stuck in a cycle where chronic illness raises cortisol, and elevated cortisol exacerbates the symptoms of the disease.

Exercise and Cortisol: Finding the Right Balance

Exercise is another common physical stressor that triggers cortisol release. This might sound counterintuitive, as exercise is generally considered a healthy activity that reduces stress. However, intense physical activity causes a temporary spike in cortisol because the body perceives exercise as a form of stress that requires energy and resources.

High-Intensity Exercise and Cortisol Spikes

For individuals engaging in high-intensity workouts, such as CrossFit, long-distance running, or weightlifting, cortisol levels can rise significantly during exercise. This is because the body needs quick energy, and cortisol facilitates the release of glucose into the bloodstream.

Let's take the example of **Emma**, a competitive marathon runner. Emma follows a rigorous training schedule, often running for hours each day. While this level of physical exertion helps her maintain peak performance, it also puts her body under constant physical stress. After her workouts, Emma often finds it hard to unwind and sleep, and she's noticed that she's gained weight around her abdomen despite maintaining a strict diet. These symptoms are classic signs of **overtraining**, where prolonged high cortisol levels from excessive exercise disrupt the body's natural recovery process.

To combat the effects of elevated cortisol, Emma's coach recommended she incorporate more rest days, focus on recovery through yoga and stretching, and ensure that she's getting enough sleep. Over time, these changes helped Emma reduce her cortisol levels and improve her performance.

Low-Intensity Exercise and Cortisol Reduction

On the other hand, **low-intensity exercise**, such as walking, yoga, or light swimming, has been shown to **reduce cortisol levels**. These types of activities activate the parasympathetic nervous system, which promotes relaxation and helps lower stress hormones.

In contrast to Emma, **Sophie**, a 50-year-old office worker, decided to take up yoga to help manage her stress levels. After a few months of regular practice, she noticed improvements in her mood, sleep, and overall well-being. Her cortisol levels, which had been elevated due to the chronic stress of her job, started to normalize, and she felt more energized throughout the day.

The takeaway here is that exercise is a powerful tool for managing cortisol, but it's important to find the right balance. While high-intensity workouts can temporarily spike cortisol, incorporating rest and low-intensity activities can help keep cortisol levels in check.

2.2

Psychological Stressors: Anxiety, Trauma, and Chronic Stress

Psychological stress is perhaps the most well-known trigger for elevated cortisol. Whether you're dealing with anxiety, a traumatic experience, or chronic work-related stress, your brain perceives these situations as threats, and the body responds by releasing cortisol.

Chronic Anxiety and Cortisol

Anxiety is a major contributor to elevated cortisol. When you feel anxious, your brain is constantly on high alert, scanning for potential threats. This hypervigilance keeps the HPA axis activated, leading to frequent surges of cortisol.

Karen, a 32-year-old woman working in a high-pressure sales job, often found herself overwhelmed by anxiety. She worried constantly about meeting her sales targets, managing difficult clients, and maintaining her performance. Over time, Karen's anxiety became a constant presence, and she began experiencing physical symptoms such as heart palpitations, headaches, and digestive problems. After visiting her doctor, Karen learned that her cortisol levels were consistently elevated.

Karen's experience is typical of individuals with **generalized anxiety disorder (GAD)**, where anxiety is ever-present and often irrational. For people like Karen, therapy, relaxation techniques, and lifestyle changes can help reduce anxiety and lower cortisol levels.

Trauma and Post-Traumatic Stress Disorder (PTSD)

Traumatic experiences can have a profound effect on cortisol levels, often leading to long-term dysregulation of the HPA axis. In cases of **post-traumatic stress disorder (PTSD)**, individuals experience chronic stress, nightmares, flashbacks, and emotional numbness, all of which are associated with elevated cortisol.

David, a 45-year-old military veteran, developed PTSD after serving in a war zone. Despite being removed from the traumatic environment, David's brain continued to perceive danger, and his cortisol levels remained elevated. This chronic state of stress contributed to insomnia, irritability, and difficulty concentrating.

To manage his PTSD, David underwent therapy and started practicing mindfulness meditation, which helped calm his nervous system and reduce cortisol levels. Although the road to recovery was long, David was able to regain control over his stress response with time and support.

2.3
Lifestyle Factors: Sleep Deprivation, Diet, and Stimulants

Lifestyle choices have a significant impact on cortisol levels. Factors like poor sleep, an unhealthy diet, and excessive caffeine or sugar consumption can all contribute to elevated cortisol.

The Role of Sleep in Cortisol Regulation

Sleep is crucial for regulating cortisol. Cortisol levels follow a natural rhythm known as the **circadian rhythm**, where they are highest in the morning and gradually decrease throughout the day. However, poor sleep or sleep deprivation can disrupt this rhythm, leading to elevated cortisol levels that make it harder to fall asleep, creating a vicious cycle.

Tom, a 40-year-old software engineer, often worked late into the night and rarely got more than five hours of sleep. He started feeling constantly exhausted, irritable, and noticed that he was gaining weight around his midsection. After consulting a sleep specialist, Tom learned that his erratic sleep schedule was causing his cortisol levels to spike in the evening, which disrupted his ability to sleep well.

By making simple changes—such as setting a consistent bedtime, reducing screen time before bed, and creating a relaxing evening routine—Tom was able to improve his sleep and reduce his cortisol levels.

Diet: How Food Affects Cortisol

What you eat plays a crucial role in regulating cortisol. Certain foods, particularly those high in sugar and refined carbohydrates, can cause blood sugar levels to spike and crash, triggering cortisol release to stabilize them.

Jane, a 28-year-old office assistant, had a habit of eating sugary snacks throughout the day to stay energized. However, she found that she was often hungry and irritable within a couple of hours. Her diet of processed foods was causing her blood sugar levels to fluctuate, leading to cortisol surges. After switching to a more balanced diet—focusing on whole foods like vegetables, lean proteins, and healthy fats—Jane noticed a significant improvement in her mood and energy levels, as well as reduced stress.

Chapter 3: The Impact of Cortisol on Your Body and Mind

Cortisol is essential for survival, but when levels are too high for too long, it can wreak havoc on both your physical and mental health. In this chapter, we will explore the short-term and long-term effects of elevated cortisol, focusing on how it affects various systems in the body, including the immune system, metabolism, cardiovascular health, and mental function.

3.1
Short-Term Effects of Cortisol: The Body's Immediate Response

Cortisol's short-term effects are largely beneficial, especially when you're faced with an acute stressor. When cortisol is released, it primes your body to respond to stress by mobilizing energy, suppressing non-essential functions (such as digestion), and boosting focus. This response is critical for handling immediate challenges.

Let's look at the story of **Rachel**, a nurse working in a busy hospital. One day, Rachel was dealing with an emergency where multiple patients needed critical care. In the heat of the moment, her body responded by flooding her system with cortisol, along with other stress hormones like adrenaline. She felt hyper-focused and energized, allowing her to manage the emergency situation effectively. After the crisis was resolved, her cortisol levels dropped back to normal, allowing her to relax and recover.

In cases like Rachel's, cortisol serves a protective role. Its short-term release helps you stay alert, focused, and energized during stressful situations. Once the stressor passes, cortisol levels should return to normal. However, if stress is prolonged or repeated frequently, the body can remain in a state of heightened cortisol production, which can have damaging effects over time.

3.2
Long-Term Effects of Elevated Cortisol

When cortisol levels remain elevated for extended periods, the effects can shift from beneficial to harmful. Chronic high cortisol levels can lead to **immune suppression**, **weight gain**, **digestive issues**, and even **cognitive decline**. Let's take a closer look at the long-term impact of elevated cortisol on different systems in the body.

Immune Suppression and Increased Risk of Illness

Cortisol's anti-inflammatory effects are beneficial in the short term, but over time, high levels of cortisol can suppress the immune system. This leaves the body more vulnerable to infections and illnesses.

James, a 50-year-old high-level executive, was under immense pressure at work. He worked late hours, skipped meals, and often felt too stressed to take time off. After months of nonstop work, James started to get sick frequently—colds, flu, and even minor infections that he previously fought off easily now lingered for weeks. His doctor explained that his prolonged high cortisol levels were weakening his immune system, making it harder for his body to fight off illnesses.

In James's case, chronic stress was the main factor contributing to his weakened immune system. Elevated cortisol had suppressed his body's normal immune response, leaving him susceptible to infections. It wasn't until James began making lifestyle changes, like reducing his work hours and incorporating stress-relief techniques, that his health improved, and his cortisol levels returned to normal.

Weight Gain and Metabolic Dysfunction

One of the most well-known effects of chronic high cortisol is weight gain, especially around the abdominal area. This happens because cortisol encourages the body to store fat, particularly visceral fat, which accumulates around the organs and is linked to metabolic diseases such as Type 2 diabetes and cardiovascular disease.

Megan, a 35-year-old mother of two, began to notice she was gaining weight despite following a relatively healthy diet and exercising regularly. Most of the weight seemed to accumulate around her midsection. Megan's doctor ran some tests and found that her cortisol levels were elevated due to the chronic stress of managing a busy household, working full-time, and not getting enough sleep. The high cortisol levels were not only contributing to weight gain but also making it harder for her body to burn fat.

In Megan's case, cortisol was slowing down her metabolism and causing her body to store fat in her abdomen. The solution involved addressing her stress levels—through better time management, improving sleep, and incorporating relaxation techniques like yoga.

3.3
Cortisol's Impact on Mental Health and Brain Function

Cortisol's effects aren't limited to the body—it also has a profound impact on the brain. While small bursts of cortisol can improve focus and memory in the short term, chronic high cortisol levels can impair cognitive function, leading to problems with memory, focus, and even mental health disorders.

Memory Problems and Cognitive Decline

The **hippocampus**, a region of the brain responsible for memory and learning, is particularly sensitive to cortisol. In small amounts, cortisol can enhance memory formation, especially during stressful situations. However, when cortisol levels remain high for too long, the hippocampus becomes overexposed to the hormone, leading to damage and shrinkage.

Henry, a 60-year-old retiree, started noticing memory lapses and difficulty concentrating after several years of caring for his elderly mother. The constant stress of caregiving had left Henry feeling overwhelmed, and his doctor found that his cortisol levels were significantly elevated. Over time, the high cortisol levels had impaired his hippocampus, leading to memory problems.

Research shows that individuals with chronic high cortisol levels are more likely to develop cognitive decline and conditions like Alzheimer's disease. In Henry's case, his memory problems were directly related to the prolonged exposure of his brain to high levels of cortisol. By addressing his stress through therapy and incorporating mindfulness practices, Henry was able to lower his cortisol levels and improve his cognitive function.

Anxiety, Depression, and Mood Swings

Cortisol also affects the **amygdala**, the part of the brain responsible for processing emotions like fear and anxiety. High cortisol levels can make the amygdala more sensitive, leading to heightened feelings of anxiety and irritability. Over time, this can contribute to the development of mood disorders like anxiety and depression.

Sophia, a 28-year-old graduate student, was struggling with overwhelming anxiety as she worked on her thesis. She found herself constantly worrying, feeling on edge, and unable to relax, even during downtime. A visit to her therapist revealed that Sophia's cortisol levels were elevated due to the chronic stress of managing her academic workload. The high cortisol was not only contributing to her anxiety but also disrupting her sleep, creating a vicious cycle.

Through a combination of therapy, meditation, and a more balanced schedule, Sophia was able to lower her cortisol levels and reduce her anxiety. Her therapist explained that managing stress was crucial not only for her mental health but also for preventing long-term damage to her brain's emotional processing centers.

Burnout and Fatigue

When cortisol levels remain elevated for too long, the body's adrenal glands can become overworked, leading to a condition known as **adrenal fatigue**. In this state, the adrenal glands struggle to produce enough cortisol, leaving you feeling exhausted and unable to handle stress.

Lisa, a 45-year-old high school teacher, started noticing that she was feeling tired all the time, even after a full night's sleep. She had been juggling a demanding teaching schedule, raising two children, and managing her household for years, but lately, she found it harder and harder to keep up. After consulting with her doctor, she learned that her adrenal glands were burned out from years of producing high levels of cortisol.

Lisa's experience is common among individuals who experience chronic stress without adequate rest or recovery. Adrenal fatigue leaves you feeling tired, unmotivated, and unable to cope with even minor stressors. The solution lies in making lifestyle changes, such as getting more rest, reducing stressors, and incorporating more relaxing activities into daily life.

3.4
Long-Term Health Risks: Cardiovascular Disease, Diabetes, and More

Chronic elevated cortisol levels not only affect mental health and brain function but can also have serious long-term consequences for physical health. High cortisol has been linked to **cardiovascular disease**, **Type 2 diabetes**, and **osteoporosis**, among other conditions.

Cardiovascular Disease

One of the most concerning long-term effects of elevated cortisol is its impact on heart health. Cortisol raises blood pressure and heart rate to prepare the body for action, but when this response is activated too frequently, it puts strain on the cardiovascular system.

Robert, a 55-year-old lawyer, had been dealing with chronic stress for most of his career. Long hours at the office, the pressure to meet clients' expectations, and his high-stakes job led to constant high cortisol levels. Over time, Robert developed high blood pressure and high cholesterol, both of which increased his risk of heart disease. His doctor explained that the chronic stress was a significant contributor to his cardiovascular problems.

For individuals like Robert, managing stress is a critical part of maintaining heart health. Reducing cortisol levels through stress management techniques, improving diet, and incorporating regular exercise can lower the risk of heart disease and stroke.

Type 2 Diabetes

Cortisol plays a key role in regulating blood sugar levels by stimulating the production of glucose. When cortisol levels remain elevated, the body becomes less responsive to insulin, which can lead to insulin resistance and, eventually, **Type 2 diabetes**.

Alex, a 40-year-old entrepreneur, had always maintained a busy lifestyle, but the stress of running his business started to take a toll on his health. He noticed that he was gaining weight, especially around his abdomen, and that he often felt fatigued after meals. His doctor diagnosed him with pre-diabetes and explained that his high cortisol levels were contributing to insulin resistance.

In cases like Alex's, managing cortisol is essential for preventing the progression from insulin resistance to full-blown diabetes. By making dietary changes, exercising regularly, and addressing the underlying stressors, Alex was able to lower his cortisol levels and improve his insulin sensitivity.

3.5
Conclusion: The Importance of Managing Cortisol for Long-Term Health

Cortisol plays a vital role in managing stress and helping the body cope with challenges, but when cortisol levels remain elevated for too long, the consequences can be serious. From immune suppression to weight gain, cognitive decline, and increased risk of chronic diseases, the impact of chronic high cortisol levels cannot be overstated.

By understanding the effects of cortisol on your body and mind, you can take proactive steps to manage your stress and prevent long-term health issues. In the following chapters, we'll explore practical strategies for lowering cortisol, including dietary changes, exercise, sleep improvements, and stress management techniques.

Chapter 4:
Nutrition and Cortisol: The Power of Food

What you eat plays a significant role in regulating cortisol levels. Certain foods can help lower cortisol and reduce stress, while others can trigger cortisol spikes, contributing to inflammation, weight gain, and fatigue. In this chapter, we'll explore how your diet influences cortisol and provide practical tips for eating in a way that supports balanced hormone levels.

4.1
The Connection Between Food and Cortisol

Your diet affects nearly every aspect of your health, including the production and regulation of hormones like cortisol. When you're under stress, your body requires more energy, and cortisol helps by mobilizing glucose (sugar) from your body's stores. This process is helpful in short bursts, but when cortisol levels are elevated for long periods, it can lead to issues like insulin resistance, weight gain, and inflammation.

Conversely, eating a balanced diet can help regulate cortisol by stabilizing blood sugar levels, reducing inflammation, and supporting the body's natural stress response.

Let's take the example of **Sarah**, a 30-year-old graphic designer. Sarah often felt stressed and exhausted after long days at work, and she frequently turned to sugary snacks and caffeine to keep her energy up throughout the day. However, instead of feeling better, Sarah noticed that she was gaining weight around her midsection and often felt jittery and anxious. After consulting a nutritionist, Sarah learned that her diet—high in sugar and caffeine—was causing her cortisol levels to spike, contributing to her stress and fatigue.

Through simple changes, like reducing her sugar intake and incorporating more whole foods into her diet, Sarah was able to lower her cortisol levels, stabilize her energy, and improve her overall well-being.

4.2
Foods That Increase Cortisol

Let's start by identifying some of the main foods and dietary habits that can cause cortisol levels to rise. While these foods may provide temporary relief or energy, they often lead to blood sugar spikes and crashes, triggering cortisol release to stabilize your body.

Refined Sugars and Processed Foods

One of the biggest contributors to elevated cortisol is a diet high in **refined sugars** and **processed foods**. These foods cause rapid spikes in blood sugar, which in turn trigger insulin release to bring blood sugar levels back down. This rapid fluctuation stresses the body and prompts the release of cortisol to maintain balance.

John, a 45-year-old accountant, relied heavily on processed snacks like chips and candy during his long workdays. He found that these foods gave him a quick energy boost, but he often crashed afterward, feeling more tired and irritable than before. His doctor explained that these blood sugar spikes were stressing his body, leading to elevated cortisol levels.

Processed foods are typically low in nutrients and high in empty calories, sugar, and unhealthy fats. This not only contributes to weight gain but also puts the body in a state of chronic stress, elevating cortisol. By switching to nutrient-dense foods like fruits, vegetables, and whole grains, John was able to reduce his cortisol levels and feel more energized throughout the day.

Caffeine and Cortisol: A Double-Edged Sword

Caffeine is another common stimulant that can raise cortisol levels. While a cup of coffee or tea can provide a short-term energy boost, excessive caffeine can keep cortisol levels elevated for hours, especially if consumed later in the day.

Case Study: Julia's Morning Coffee Habit

Julia, a 35-year-old lawyer, started her day with two cups of coffee to wake up and feel alert. As the day progressed, she often reached for more caffeine to power through her afternoon slump. However, Julia began experiencing difficulty sleeping, and she noticed that she often felt anxious or jittery. Her doctor suggested that her caffeine intake was contributing to elevated cortisol, especially since she was drinking coffee late into the afternoon.

By cutting back on caffeine and switching to herbal teas in the afternoon, Julia noticed improvements in her sleep and mood. She felt more balanced and less anxious as her cortisol levels stabilized.

To avoid caffeine's cortisol-boosting effects, it's best to limit consumption, particularly in the afternoon and evening when it can disrupt your sleep and lead to prolonged high cortisol levels.

High-Sodium Foods

While cortisol regulates salt and water balance in the body, diets that are excessively high in sodium can also lead to elevated cortisol levels. This is because high-sodium diets can raise blood pressure, triggering the body's stress response.

Practical Tip: Reducing Sodium Intake

Cutting back on processed foods, canned soups, and salty snacks can help keep cortisol levels in check. Instead, focus on fresh ingredients and season meals with herbs and spices rather than salt.

4.3
Foods That Lower Cortisol

Fortunately, there are many foods that can help lower cortisol levels by supporting your body's natural stress response. These foods typically have anti-inflammatory properties, are rich in vitamins and minerals, and help stabilize blood sugar levels.

Complex Carbohydrates and Whole Grains

Unlike refined carbohydrates (like white bread and sugary snacks), **complex carbohydrates** provide a steady release of energy and help prevent blood sugar spikes and crashes. Whole grains like oats, quinoa, and brown rice are particularly good at stabilizing blood sugar and preventing cortisol spikes.

Megan's Experience with Whole Grains Megan, a busy teacher, often skipped breakfast or grabbed a sugary pastry on the go. She found that she was constantly hungry by mid-morning and often felt shaky or lightheaded. After speaking with a nutritionist, Megan switched to a more balanced breakfast, including oatmeal with nuts and seeds. This change not only helped stabilize her blood sugar throughout the day but also reduced her stress levels as her cortisol remained more balanced.

Complex carbohydrates are a great way to keep your energy stable and reduce stress, especially when combined with protein and healthy fats.

Healthy Fats: Omega-3 Fatty Acids

Healthy fats, particularly **Omega-3 fatty acids**, are known for their anti-inflammatory properties and their ability to reduce cortisol levels. Omega-3s, found in fatty fish (like salmon, mackerel, and sardines), walnuts, flaxseeds, and chia seeds, help protect the body from inflammation, which is often a trigger for cortisol release.

Case Study: Mark's Omega-3 Supplementation

Mark, a 50-year-old entrepreneur, struggled with chronic inflammation due to arthritis. His doctor recommended incorporating more Omega-3-rich foods into his diet to help lower both his inflammation and his cortisol levels. After a few months of regularly eating fatty fish and supplementing with fish oil, Mark noticed that his joint pain decreased, and his stress levels became more manageable.

Adding Omega-3s to your diet can have a profound impact on both physical and mental health by reducing cortisol and promoting overall well-being.

Leafy Greens and Vegetables

Vegetables, especially **leafy greens** like spinach, kale, and Swiss chard, are packed with magnesium, a mineral that plays a key role in regulating cortisol. Low levels of magnesium have been linked to higher cortisol levels and increased feelings of stress.

Sarah's Magnesium Boost Sarah, a college student preparing for final exams, often felt overwhelmed and anxious. Her diet lacked vegetables, and she often ate fast food between study sessions. After reading about the benefits of magnesium, Sarah started incorporating more leafy greens into her meals and even added a magnesium supplement to her routine. She found that her stress levels decreased, and she was better able to focus during her study sessions.

Magnesium-rich foods like spinach, avocados, and nuts are essential for balancing cortisol and managing stress.

Antioxidant-Rich Fruits: Berries and Citrus

Berries, such as blueberries, strawberries, and raspberries, are loaded with antioxidants that help neutralize free radicals and reduce inflammation, both of which are contributors to elevated cortisol. Similarly, citrus fruits like oranges and grapefruits provide a good dose of **vitamin C**, which has been shown to lower cortisol levels during stress.

Case Study: Emily's Antioxidant Boost

Emily, a 40-year-old business owner, often skipped lunch and snacked on processed foods throughout the day. She frequently felt tired and stressed but didn't have time to cook elaborate meals. After learning about the benefits of antioxidants, Emily started incorporating more berries into her diet by adding them to her morning smoothies and afternoon snacks. This simple change helped Emily feel more energized, and she noticed a significant reduction in her stress levels.

Incorporating more fruits rich in antioxidants and vitamin C is an easy and delicious way to support cortisol balance.

4.4
Practical Meal Planning for Lower Cortisol

Now that we've explored the types of foods that can help regulate cortisol levels, let's look at how you can create a daily meal plan that supports balanced cortisol. Incorporating these nutrient-dense foods into your diet can help stabilize your energy, reduce stress, and improve overall well-being.

Sample Cortisol-Lowering Meal Plan

Breakfast:

- Oatmeal topped with fresh berries, chia seeds, and a drizzle of almond butter.

- A cup of green tea or herbal tea (avoid caffeine-heavy drinks like coffee if possible).

Mid-Morning Snack:

- A handful of mixed nuts (almonds, walnuts) and an apple or orange.

Lunch:

- Grilled salmon (or other fatty fish) served with quinoa and a spinach salad topped with avocado and olive oil.

Afternoon Snack:

- A handful of baby carrots with hummus or a green smoothie with spinach, banana, and a spoonful of almond butter.

Dinner:

- Baked chicken with roasted sweet potatoes and steamed broccoli.

- Herbal tea (like chamomile or peppermint) to promote relaxation.

This meal plan is rich in complex carbohydrates, healthy fats, lean proteins, and antioxidants, all of which help reduce cortisol and provide the body with steady energy throughout the day.

4.5
Supplements for Cortisol Regulation

In addition to a balanced diet, certain **supplements** can support cortisol regulation. While it's always best to get nutrients from whole foods, supplements can provide additional support, particularly when dealing with chronic stress.

Ashwagandha: An Adaptogenic Herb

Ashwagandha is an adaptogenic herb that has been shown to lower cortisol levels and help the body manage stress more effectively. Adaptogens are natural substances that help the body adapt to stress and normalize bodily processes.

Paul's Experience with Ashwagandha Paul, a 35-year-old project manager, often felt stressed and overwhelmed by his workload. After researching natural ways to manage stress, he decided to try ashwagandha supplements. After several weeks, Paul noticed that he felt more calm and less anxious, even during busy periods at work. His cortisol levels also dropped, as confirmed by a follow-up test with his doctor.

Ashwagandha can be a helpful addition to a stress-management plan, particularly for individuals dealing with chronic stress.

Magnesium: A Key Mineral for Stress Relief

As mentioned earlier, **magnesium** plays an important role in regulating cortisol and reducing stress. If your diet is lacking in magnesium-rich foods, taking a magnesium supplement may help support balanced cortisol levels.

Practical Tip: Magnesium Supplements

Magnesium supplements are widely available, and taking 200–400 mg per day can be beneficial for individuals experiencing high cortisol levels or frequent stress.

4.6
Conclusion: The Power of Food in Managing Cortisol

What you eat plays a crucial role in managing cortisol levels and overall stress. By focusing on whole, nutrient-dense foods and avoiding refined sugars, processed foods, and excessive caffeine, you can support your body's natural stress response and reduce cortisol levels.

Incorporating foods rich in complex carbohydrates, healthy fats, leafy greens, and antioxidants into your daily meals can help keep your cortisol levels in balance, improve your energy, and reduce the harmful effects of stress.

In the next chapter, we'll explore the role of exercise in cortisol regulation and how to find the right balance between activity and recovery to keep stress levels in check.

Chapter 5:
Exercise and Cortisol: Finding the Right Balance

Exercise is one of the most effective ways to manage stress, improve mood, and boost overall health. However, the relationship between exercise and cortisol is a bit more complex than it seems. While regular physical activity can help lower cortisol levels in the long run, intense or excessive exercise can lead to spikes in cortisol, potentially causing more harm than good.

In this chapter, we'll explore how different types of exercise affect cortisol, the importance of rest and recovery, and how to strike the right balance to keep cortisol levels in check while reaping the benefits of physical activity.

5.1
How Exercise Impacts Cortisol Levels

When you exercise, your body perceives the physical exertion as a form of stress, which leads to a temporary increase in cortisol. This cortisol spike is your body's way of providing you with the energy needed to sustain the activity. However, the long-term effects of exercise on cortisol levels depend on the type, intensity, and duration of the exercise, as well as how well your body recovers afterward.

Short-Term Cortisol Spikes: Necessary for Performance

Let's take the example of **Matt**, a 30-year-old athlete training for a triathlon. During his high-intensity workouts, such as long-distance cycling and running, Matt's cortisol levels would rise sharply. This is a normal response, as cortisol helps mobilize glucose, providing Matt's muscles and brain with the energy required to push through the strenuous activity.

In Matt's case, the cortisol spike is necessary for optimal performance, and it helps his body adapt to the increased demands of training. However, the key to maintaining balanced cortisol levels lies in what happens after the workout. If Matt gives his body sufficient time to recover, his cortisol levels will gradually return to normal, allowing his body to repair and strengthen.

5.2
High-Intensity Exercise and Overtraining: When Cortisol Becomes a Problem

While cortisol spikes are a natural part of high-intensity exercise, problems arise when the body doesn't have enough time to recover, leading to chronic cortisol elevation. This condition is often referred to as **overtraining** or **exercise-induced stress**, and it can cause fatigue, weight gain, and burnout.

Emily's Struggle with Overtraining Emily, a 25-year-old fitness enthusiast, loved pushing her body to the limit. She worked out six days a week, combining high-intensity interval training (HIIT) with strength training and long cardio sessions. At first, Emily saw great results—she lost weight, built muscle, and felt more confident. However, after several months of intense exercise with little rest, Emily started to experience symptoms of overtraining. She felt constantly fatigued, had difficulty sleeping, and noticed that her weight loss plateaued despite sticking to her routine.

Emily's doctor explained that her body was stuck in a state of chronic stress, with cortisol levels that remained elevated throughout the day. Instead of allowing her body to recover, her rigorous workout schedule was leading to **cortisol dysregulation**, which was affecting her metabolism and sleep.

Signs of Overtraining

- Constant fatigue or low energy
- Difficulty sleeping or insomnia
- Increased appetite and cravings for sugary or fatty foods
- Plateau in fitness progress or performance
- Persistent soreness or muscle pain
- Mood swings, irritability, or increased anxiety

In cases like Emily's, the solution often involves reducing the intensity of workouts and increasing rest days to allow cortisol levels to normalize. Incorporating low-intensity activities and focusing on recovery is crucial for preventing the negative effects of overtraining.

5.3
Low-Intensity Exercise: A Tool for Lowering Cortisol

While high-intensity workouts can spike cortisol, **low-intensity exercise**—such as walking, yoga, and swimming—has been shown to reduce cortisol levels and promote relaxation. These types of activities activate the **parasympathetic nervous system**, often referred to as the "rest and digest" system, which helps lower stress hormones and calm the body.

The Benefits of Low-Intensity Exercise

Case Study: Laura's Yoga Journey

Laura, a 40-year-old marketing manager, had been struggling with chronic stress and anxiety for years. She often felt tense, and her job left her feeling mentally drained by the end of each day. After speaking with a therapist, Laura decided to incorporate yoga into her daily routine. Over time, she noticed that her stress levels decreased, and she felt more centered and relaxed.

Yoga, as well as other forms of low-intensity exercise like tai chi, walking, or gentle stretching, can help reduce cortisol levels by promoting a state of relaxation. These activities encourage mindfulness, improve breathing, and enhance blood flow, all of which help lower cortisol and improve mental clarity.

5.4
The Importance of Rest and Recovery

No matter how dedicated you are to your fitness routine, rest and recovery are just as important as the workouts themselves. Without adequate recovery, cortisol levels can remain elevated, leading to fatigue, burnout, and even injury.

The Science of Recovery

During exercise, especially intense workouts, your body experiences physical stress in the form of microscopic muscle damage, energy depletion, and an increase in cortisol. Recovery is the period during which your body repairs and replenishes itself, allowing muscles to grow stronger and cortisol levels to return to normal.

Inadequate recovery leads to a state of chronic stress, with persistently elevated cortisol levels. This not only impairs muscle growth but also affects sleep, mood, and metabolism.

Case Study: Kevin's Journey to Recovery

Kevin, a 38-year-old professional basketball player, had always pushed himself to the limit during training. However, after a grueling season, he noticed that his performance was starting to decline. He felt constantly fatigued, was more prone to injury, and his mood had taken a nosedive. After consulting with his coach and a sports psychologist, Kevin realized that he wasn't giving his body enough time to recover between training sessions. By incorporating more rest days, focusing on sleep, and adding recovery techniques like massage and stretching, Kevin was able to bounce back and improve both his performance and his overall well-being.

Rest Days and Active Recovery

Rest days are crucial for allowing cortisol levels to return to baseline. On these days, it's important to avoid intense physical exertion and focus on activities that promote relaxation, such as walking, stretching, or light yoga. **Active recovery** is another option, which involves engaging in low-intensity exercise to promote blood flow and help the body recover more quickly.

Incorporating at least one or two rest days into your weekly workout routine is essential for maintaining balanced cortisol levels and preventing burnout.

5.5
Designing a Cortisol-Friendly Exercise Routine

Finding the right balance between intense workouts and rest is key to maintaining healthy cortisol levels. Below is a guide for creating a cortisol-friendly exercise routine that supports stress management and overall well-being.

1. Include a Mix of Low- and High-Intensity Workouts

Incorporating both high-intensity and low-intensity exercises into your weekly routine ensures that you're getting the benefits of cortisol spikes for performance while also allowing time for recovery and cortisol reduction.

Sample Weekly Routine:

- **Monday:** High-intensity interval training (HIIT) for 30 minutes
- **Tuesday:** Rest day or active recovery (gentle stretching or yoga)
- **Wednesday:** Strength training (moderate intensity)
- **Thursday:** Low-intensity cardio (walking, swimming, or cycling)
- **Friday:** Rest day or restorative yoga

- **Saturday:** High-intensity cardio (running, cycling)
- **Sunday:** Low-intensity yoga or tai chi

2. Prioritize Rest and Recovery

Make sure to incorporate at least one or two rest days each week. On these days, focus on relaxation, sleep, and light activity to allow your body to recover.

3. Listen to Your Body

Pay attention to signs of overtraining, such as fatigue, irritability, or difficulty sleeping. If you notice these signs, consider adjusting the intensity of your workouts and increasing your recovery time.

Practical Tip: Heart Rate Monitoring

Using a heart rate monitor can help you gauge the intensity of your workouts and ensure that you're staying within a healthy range. Over time, this can prevent overtraining and help you maintain balanced cortisol levels.

5.6
Conclusion: Exercise as a Tool for Cortisol Management

Exercise is one of the most powerful tools for managing cortisol, but it's important to strike the right balance. While high-intensity workouts can temporarily spike cortisol levels, they are beneficial when followed by adequate rest and recovery. On the other hand, low-intensity exercises like yoga and walking can help reduce cortisol levels and promote relaxation.

By designing a balanced exercise routine that includes both intense and restorative activities, you can keep your cortisol levels in check, improve your fitness, and reduce the harmful effects of chronic stress. In the next chapter, we'll explore the role of sleep in cortisol regulation and provide practical tips for improving your sleep habits to support balanced cortisol levels.

Chapter 6:
The Importance of Sleep: Resting Your Way to Hormonal Balance

Sleep is one of the most critical factors in regulating cortisol and maintaining overall health. The relationship between sleep and cortisol is bidirectional: just as cortisol impacts the quality of your sleep, your sleep patterns influence cortisol production. In this chapter, we'll explore how sleep regulates cortisol, the effects of sleep deprivation on your body, and practical strategies for improving your sleep to maintain balanced cortisol levels.

6.1
The Circadian Rhythm and Cortisol Production

Your body follows a natural **circadian rhythm**, which is a 24-hour internal clock that governs various physiological processes, including sleep, energy levels, and hormone production. Cortisol plays a key role in this rhythm, rising and falling at specific times throughout the day to keep you awake, alert, and relaxed when needed.

Cortisol's Natural Daily Cycle

Cortisol levels are typically highest in the morning, helping you wake up and feel alert. This early morning spike, known as the **cortisol awakening response (CAR)**, prepares your body for the day ahead by mobilizing energy and increasing blood sugar levels. As the day progresses, cortisol levels gradually decline, reaching their lowest point in the evening to help you unwind and sleep.

Let's take the example of **Michael**, a 35-year-old software developer. Michael's job required him to be alert and focused during early-morning meetings. His body naturally produced more cortisol in the mornings to help him stay sharp and energized. By evening, his cortisol levels would drop, signaling that it was time to relax and get ready for bed.

In a healthy individual like Michael, cortisol follows this natural rhythm, peaking in the morning and gradually tapering off throughout the day. This rhythm allows for periods of high energy and productivity, followed by rest and recovery. However, when the circadian rhythm is disrupted—due to poor sleep habits or external stressors—cortisol levels can become dysregulated, leading to long-term health problems.

Disruptions to the Circadian Rhythm

There are many factors that can disrupt the circadian rhythm and, consequently, cortisol production. These include:

- **Sleep deprivation**
- **Shift work or irregular sleep schedules**
- **Chronic stress**
- **Excessive screen time or exposure to blue light in the evening**
- **Travel across time zones (jet lag)**

Let's consider **Anna**, a 42-year-old nurse who worked night shifts. Her irregular sleep schedule caused her cortisol levels to become imbalanced. Instead of following the normal rise-and-fall pattern, Anna's cortisol levels stayed elevated throughout the day and night, making it difficult for her to fall asleep during her off hours. Over time, this disrupted rhythm led to chronic fatigue, weight gain, and mood swings.

6.2
The Effects of Sleep Deprivation on Cortisol Levels

Sleep deprivation is one of the most common causes of elevated cortisol. When you don't get enough sleep, your body perceives this as a form of stress, leading to an increase in cortisol production. Over time, chronic sleep deprivation can result in a state of **cortisol dysregulation**, where cortisol levels remain elevated even during times of rest.

The Sleep-Cortisol Cycle

The relationship between sleep and cortisol is cyclical. Poor sleep leads to elevated cortisol levels, and elevated cortisol levels make it harder to sleep. This creates a **vicious cycle** where individuals become trapped in a pattern of poor sleep and high stress, leading to long-term health consequences.

Let's look at the story of **Tom**, a 50-year-old sales executive. Tom's job required him to travel frequently, often across multiple time zones. He rarely got more than five hours of sleep each night and found himself feeling stressed and fatigued. As his sleep quality worsened, his cortisol levels remained high throughout the day, making it difficult for him to wind down in the evenings. Tom's sleep deprivation led to higher cortisol levels, which in turn made it harder for him to fall asleep—a cycle that took a toll on both his physical and mental health.

The Long-Term Effects of Sleep Deprivation on Health

Chronic sleep deprivation and elevated cortisol levels can lead to serious long-term health problems, including:

- **Weight gain**: Elevated cortisol stimulates appetite and encourages the body to store fat, particularly around the abdomen.

- **Increased risk of cardiovascular disease**: High cortisol levels contribute to high blood pressure and inflammation, both of which increase the risk of heart disease.

- **Insulin resistance and Type 2 diabetes**: Cortisol raises blood sugar levels, and chronic sleep deprivation can lead to insulin resistance, increasing the risk of diabetes.

- **Cognitive decline**: Elevated cortisol can damage the hippocampus, leading to memory problems and cognitive decline over time.

Tom's story is a clear example of how sleep deprivation can contribute to long-term health risks. By addressing his sleep patterns and finding ways to reduce stress, Tom was able to break the cycle and improve his overall health.

6.3
Practical Tips for Improving Sleep and Regulating Cortisol

Improving your sleep quality is one of the most effective ways to regulate cortisol levels and reduce stress. Below are practical tips that can help you improve your sleep habits and support balanced cortisol production.

1. Stick to a Consistent Sleep Schedule

Going to bed and waking up at the same time each day helps regulate your circadian rhythm and ensures that cortisol follows its natural cycle. Even on weekends, it's important to maintain a consistent schedule to keep your internal clock in sync.

Practical Tip: Aim to go to bed within the same 30-minute window every night. Set an alarm to remind yourself when it's time to wind down and start your bedtime routine.

2. Create a Relaxing Bedtime Routine

Establishing a calming pre-sleep routine can signal to your body that it's time to unwind and prepare for rest. This routine could include:

- Reading a book

- Practicing relaxation techniques (such as deep breathing or meditation)
- Taking a warm bath
- Listening to calming music or nature sounds

Case Study: Emma's Bedtime Routine

Emma, a 28-year-old teacher, struggled with winding down after busy workdays. She often found herself lying in bed, scrolling through her phone, which left her feeling more anxious and alert. After speaking with a sleep specialist, Emma developed a bedtime routine that included reading a book and doing a 10-minute meditation before bed. Over time, she noticed that she fell asleep more easily and felt more rested in the morning.

---

3. Limit Screen Time and Blue Light Exposure

Blue light emitted by phones, tablets, and computers can interfere with melatonin production, the hormone responsible for regulating sleep. Limiting screen time, especially in the evening, can help improve sleep quality and reduce cortisol levels.

Practical Tip: Try to avoid screens for at least one hour before bedtime. Instead, opt for relaxing activities like reading or journaling. If you need to use a device in the evening, consider using blue light filters or wearing blue light-blocking glasses.

---

4. Optimize Your Sleep Environment

Your sleep environment plays a crucial role in determining the quality of your rest. Ensuring that your bedroom is comfortable, quiet, and conducive to sleep can help you fall asleep faster and stay asleep longer.

Tips for Optimizing Your Sleep Environment:

- **Keep your room cool**: A temperature of around 60-67°F (15-19°C) is ideal for sleep.

- **Use blackout curtains**: Darkness signals to your body that it's time to sleep, helping regulate melatonin production.

- **Minimize noise**: Use earplugs, white noise machines, or calming sounds to drown out any disruptive noise.

- **Invest in a comfortable mattress and pillows**: Your sleep quality depends on your comfort, so make sure your bed is supportive and comfortable.

Case Study: James's Sleep Makeover

James, a 45-year-old business owner, often woke up in the middle of the night due to noise from the street outside his apartment. His bedroom was also cluttered with work papers, making it difficult for him to relax. After a sleep expert suggested changes, James invested in blackout curtains, started using a white noise machine, and decluttered his room. These simple changes helped him sleep more soundly and reduced his nighttime cortisol levels.

---

5. Practice Relaxation Techniques Before Bed

Relaxation techniques can help lower cortisol levels and prepare your body for rest. Techniques like deep breathing, progressive muscle relaxation, and guided meditation are excellent tools for calming the mind and body before sleep.

Practical Tip: Try practicing a simple breathing exercise called **4-7-8 breathing** before bed. Here's how it works:

- Inhale for a count of 4.
- Hold your breath for a count of 7.
- Exhale slowly for a count of 8.
- Repeat this cycle 4-5 times to reduce stress and promote relaxation.

6. Avoid Stimulants Late in the Day

Caffeine and other stimulants can interfere with your ability to fall asleep and cause cortisol levels to spike. Try to avoid caffeine in the late afternoon and evening to ensure that it doesn't disrupt your sleep.

Practical Tip: If you enjoy coffee or tea, try switching to decaffeinated options in the afternoon and evening. Herbal teas like chamomile or peppermint can also promote relaxation and help you wind down before bed.

7. Incorporate Natural Sleep Aids if Needed

If you're struggling with sleep despite making lifestyle changes, you may consider incorporating natural sleep aids, such as melatonin supplements or magnesium, which can help regulate sleep patterns and reduce cortisol levels.

Case Study: Sophie's Melatonin Supplement

Sophie, a 50-year-old caregiver, found it difficult to sleep after caring for her elderly mother all day. Her stress levels were high, and she often lay awake at night, feeling restless. After speaking with her doctor, Sophie began taking a small dose of melatonin before bed, which helped her fall asleep more easily. With improved sleep, her cortisol levels began to normalize, and she felt more energetic and focused during the day.

6.4
Conclusion: Prioritizing Sleep for Cortisol Balance

Sleep is one of the most powerful tools for regulating cortisol and maintaining overall health. By understanding the relationship between sleep and cortisol and making practical changes to improve your sleep habits, you can break the cycle of stress and sleep deprivation, leading to better physical and mental health.

Prioritizing consistent sleep patterns, creating a relaxing bedtime routine, and optimizing your sleep environment can all contribute to better sleep quality and lower cortisol levels. In the next chapter, we'll explore **stress management techniques**, including mindfulness and relaxation practices, that can further help reduce cortisol and improve your well-being.

Chapter 7:
Stress Management Techniques: Lowering Cortisol Through Mindfulness and Relaxation

Stress is one of the primary triggers of elevated cortisol, but the good news is that there are many effective techniques to reduce stress and lower cortisol levels. In this chapter, we'll explore a variety of stress management practices that have been scientifically proven to help calm the mind, relax the body, and support cortisol balance. From mindfulness and meditation to yoga and deep breathing, these techniques can be easily incorporated into your daily routine to reduce cortisol and improve your overall well-being.

7.1
Mindfulness and Meditation: The Power of Being Present

Mindfulness is the practice of bringing your attention to the present moment without judgment. It involves being fully aware of your thoughts, feelings, and surroundings, while letting go of distractions and stressors. Numerous studies have shown that mindfulness practices, especially when combined with meditation, can significantly reduce cortisol levels and improve mental health.

How Mindfulness Reduces Cortisol

Mindfulness works by calming the **sympathetic nervous system**, which is responsible for the body's "fight or flight" response to stress. By focusing on the present moment and accepting your thoughts and feelings without judgment, mindfulness helps to reduce the body's stress response, lowering cortisol levels and promoting relaxation.

Case Study: Mark's Mindfulness Journey

Mark, a 45-year-old accountant, had been experiencing chronic stress due to long work hours and tight deadlines. He found himself feeling anxious and overwhelmed, with difficulty sleeping and concentrating. After reading about the benefits of mindfulness, Mark decided to try incorporating it into his daily routine. He began practicing mindfulness meditation for just 10 minutes each morning, focusing on his breath and letting go of any anxious thoughts. Over time, Mark noticed that he felt more calm, focused, and better able to handle stress. His doctor confirmed that his cortisol levels had dropped, and he was sleeping better than before.

Mindfulness Exercises to Lower Cortisol

You don't need to be a meditation expert to start practicing mindfulness. Here are a few simple mindfulness exercises that can help lower cortisol levels:

- **Breath Awareness**: Sit quietly and bring your attention to your breath. Focus on each inhale and exhale, and gently let go of any distracting thoughts. Whenever your mind starts to wander, bring your focus back to your breath.

- **Body Scan Meditation**: Lie down in a comfortable position and bring your awareness to different parts of your body, starting from your toes and working your way up to your head. As you scan your body, notice any areas of tension or discomfort and try to release them as you exhale.

- **Mindful Walking**: Take a walk outside, paying close attention to the sights, sounds, and sensations around you. Notice how your body feels as you walk, and focus on the rhythm of your steps and breath.

These simple mindfulness practices can be done in just a few minutes each day and can have a powerful impact on reducing stress and cortisol.

7.2
Yoga and Breathwork: Combining Movement with Relaxation

Yoga is a mind-body practice that combines physical movement, breath control, and meditation. It has been shown to lower cortisol levels, reduce anxiety, and improve mood. The physical postures (asanas) in yoga stretch and strengthen the body, while the breathwork (pranayama) and meditation promote relaxation and mental clarity.

The Cortisol-Lowering Effects of Yoga

Yoga helps reduce cortisol by activating the **parasympathetic nervous system**, often referred to as the "rest and digest" system. This part of the nervous system is responsible for counteracting the body's stress response, promoting relaxation and reducing the production of stress hormones like cortisol.

Case Study: Sarah's Yoga Practice

Sarah, a 35-year-old teacher, had been dealing with high levels of stress and anxiety due to her demanding job. She often felt tense, with frequent headaches and difficulty sleeping. After attending a few yoga classes, Sarah noticed an immediate improvement in her mood and energy levels. Over time, her regular yoga practice helped her reduce her cortisol levels, sleep better, and manage her stress more effectively.

Practical Yoga Exercises for Lowering Cortisol

Here are a few simple yoga poses and breathing exercises that can help reduce cortisol:

- **Child's Pose (Balasana)**: This gentle, resting pose helps relax the body and calm the mind. Kneel on the floor, sit back on your heels, and extend your arms forward, resting your forehead on the ground. Breathe deeply and stay in the pose for 2-3 minutes.

- **Legs-Up-the-Wall Pose (Viparita Karani)**: This restorative pose encourages blood flow to the upper body and helps lower cortisol levels. Lie on your back with your legs extended up against a wall. Relax your arms by your sides and breathe deeply, holding the pose for 5-10 minutes.

- **Alternate Nostril Breathing (Nadi Shodhana):** This simple breathing technique helps balance the nervous system and reduce stress. Sit comfortably and close your right nostril with your right thumb. Inhale slowly through your left nostril, then close your left nostril with your right ring finger. Exhale slowly through your right nostril. Repeat this cycle for 5-10 breaths, switching nostrils with each breath.

By incorporating these yoga poses and breathwork into your daily routine, you can promote relaxation, reduce stress, and lower cortisol levels naturally.

7.3
Deep Breathing Exercises: Calming the Nervous System

Breathing is one of the most effective ways to reduce cortisol quickly. Deep, slow breathing signals to your brain that you are safe and relaxed, which in turn calms the sympathetic nervous system and lowers cortisol levels.

Case Study: David's Breathing Routine

David, a 50-year-old lawyer, often found himself feeling stressed during work meetings. His heart would race, and he felt tense and anxious. A friend recommended that David try deep breathing exercises to manage his stress. By practicing deep breathing before and during stressful moments, David was able to calm his mind, lower his cortisol levels, and feel more in control.

Simple Breathing Techniques to Lower Cortisol

Here are a few simple breathing exercises that can help lower cortisol and reduce stress:

- **Box Breathing**: Inhale for a count of 4, hold your breath for 4 counts, exhale for 4 counts, and hold for another 4 counts. Repeat this cycle for 5-10 minutes to calm the mind and lower cortisol.

- **Diaphragmatic Breathing**: Place one hand on your chest and the other on your belly. Inhale deeply through your nose, allowing your belly to rise as you breathe in. Exhale slowly through your mouth, letting your belly fall. This type of deep breathing helps activate the parasympathetic nervous system and reduce stress.

These breathing exercises can be done anytime, anywhere, and are a powerful way to quickly lower cortisol and calm the nervous system.

7.4
Cognitive-Behavioral Therapy (CBT): Reframing Stressful Thoughts

Cognitive-behavioral therapy (CBT) is a psychological treatment that focuses on identifying and changing negative thought patterns that contribute to stress and anxiety. By reframing stressful thoughts and learning healthier ways to cope with challenges, CBT can help reduce cortisol levels and improve overall well-being.

How CBT Reduces Cortisol

CBT works by helping individuals recognize when their thoughts are irrational or unhelpful, and teaches them to challenge and reframe these thoughts. By reducing anxiety and promoting healthier thought patterns, CBT lowers the body's stress response, leading to a reduction in cortisol.

Case Study: Jessica's CBT Experience

Jessica, a 30-year-old social worker, often felt overwhelmed by the demands of her job. She frequently had negative thoughts about her ability to handle stress, which only made her anxiety worse. After starting CBT with a therapist, Jessica learned how to identify and reframe her negative thoughts. She practiced techniques like questioning the evidence behind her fears and replacing them with more balanced, rational thoughts. Over time, Jessica's anxiety decreased, and her therapist noted a significant reduction in her cortisol levels.

Practical CBT Techniques for Reducing Cortisol

Here are a few CBT techniques that can help manage stress and lower cortisol:

- **Thought Record**: Keep a journal of your stressful thoughts, and challenge them by asking questions like: "Is this thought based on facts or assumptions?" and "What's the worst that could realistically happen?" By examining your thoughts objectively, you can reduce anxiety and prevent cortisol spikes.

- **Cognitive Restructuring**: When you notice a negative thought, practice reframing it into a more balanced perspective. For example, instead of thinking, "I'll never get everything done," try reframing it to, "I have a lot to do, but I'll take it one step at a time."

CBT is a powerful tool for managing stress and lowering cortisol levels by changing the way you think about and respond to stressful situations.

7.5
Gratitude and Positive Thinking: Shifting Your Focus to Reduce Stress

Practicing gratitude and focusing on positive thoughts can also help reduce cortisol levels. Research has shown that individuals who regularly practice gratitude experience lower stress, better mood, and improved physical health.

The Science Behind Gratitude and Cortisol

When you focus on positive aspects of your life and practice gratitude, your brain releases feel-good chemicals like dopamine and serotonin. These chemicals counteract the effects of cortisol and promote relaxation and well-being.

Case Study: Amy's Gratitude Practice

Amy, a 45-year-old nurse, often felt stressed and burned out from her job. After attending a workshop on stress management, she started keeping a gratitude journal, writing down three things she was grateful for each day. Over time, Amy noticed that her mood improved, and she felt less overwhelmed by daily stress. Her gratitude practice helped her shift her focus away from negative thoughts, and she experienced a reduction in cortisol levels as a result.

Practical Tips for Practicing Gratitude

Here are a few simple ways to incorporate gratitude into your daily routine:

- **Gratitude Journal**: Write down three things you're grateful for each day, no matter how small. This practice can help shift your focus away from stress and negativity.

- **Gratitude Meditation**: Spend a few minutes each day reflecting on the positive aspects of your life. Focus on the things that bring you joy and peace, and let those feelings wash over you.

By regularly practicing gratitude, you can train your brain to focus on positive experiences, reducing stress and lowering cortisol levels.

7.6
Conclusion: Managing Stress to Lower Cortisol

Managing stress effectively is one of the most important factors in maintaining balanced cortisol levels and promoting overall health. By incorporating techniques like mindfulness, yoga, breathing exercises, CBT, and gratitude into your daily routine, you can reduce cortisol and feel more calm, centered, and in control of your stress.

These techniques are simple yet powerful tools that can be practiced anywhere, anytime, and can have a profound impact on both your mental and physical health. In the next chapter, we'll explore how to create an environment and lifestyle that supports low cortisol levels, from optimizing your home and workspace to managing digital stress and building strong relationships.

Chapter 8: **Environmental and Lifestyle Adjustments for Lower Cortisol**

Your surroundings and daily habits can have a profound impact on your stress levels and cortisol production. In this chapter, we'll explore how your environment—both physical and digital—affects cortisol levels and what adjustments you can make to create a cortisol-friendly lifestyle. From optimizing your home and workspace to managing digital overload, these changes can help reduce stress and support long-term well-being.

8.1
How Your Environment Affects Cortisol

Your physical environment plays a major role in how stressed or relaxed you feel throughout the day. Factors like noise, lighting, and clutter can all influence your stress response and contribute to elevated cortisol levels. By making intentional changes to your environment, you can create a more calming, supportive space that promotes relaxation and reduces stress.

Noise Pollution and Cortisol

Noise is a significant environmental stressor that can lead to elevated cortisol levels. Whether it's the sound of traffic, loud neighbors, or constant interruptions at work, noise pollution can trigger the body's stress response, keeping cortisol levels elevated.

Case Study: James and the City Noise

James, a 40-year-old financial analyst, lived in a busy city with constant noise from traffic, construction, and nightlife. He often felt tense and anxious at home, struggling to relax after long workdays. After speaking with a stress management coach, James realized that the noise in his environment was a major contributor to his elevated cortisol levels. To address this, James invested in noise-canceling headphones, added soundproof curtains to his windows, and started using a white noise machine to drown out the external sounds. These changes made a significant difference in his stress levels and helped him relax more effectively at home.

Practical Tip: To reduce noise pollution in your environment, try using noise-canceling devices, white noise machines, or earplugs. You can also create a quieter home environment by adding rugs, curtains, and other soft furnishings that absorb sound.

Lighting and Its Impact on Stress

Lighting plays a crucial role in regulating your circadian rhythm, which directly influences cortisol production. Natural light exposure helps regulate the sleep-wake cycle, while excessive exposure to artificial light—especially blue light from screens—can disrupt melatonin production and elevate cortisol levels.

Case Study: Emma's Lighting Makeover

Emma, a 28-year-old freelance writer, worked from home and often found herself staring at a computer screen for hours late into the night. Her sleep was frequently disrupted, and she felt stressed and fatigued during the day. After learning about the effects of blue light on cortisol, Emma decided to adjust her workspace. She replaced the bright overhead lights with soft, warm lighting in the evening and started using blue light-blocking glasses when working on her computer. Emma also made a habit of going for a walk outside in the morning to get natural light exposure. These changes helped regulate her circadian rhythm, lower her cortisol levels, and improve her sleep.

Practical Tip: To optimize lighting in your environment, aim to get natural sunlight exposure during the day, especially in the morning. In the evening, switch to warm, dim lighting and avoid screens for at least an hour before bed.

Clutter and Its Effect on Mental Health

Cluttered environments can lead to feelings of chaos, overwhelm, and stress, all of which can contribute to elevated cortisol levels. A cluttered space can make it difficult to focus, relax, or feel in control, leading to a constant low-level stress response.

Case Study: Laura's Clutter-Free Zone

Laura, a 32-year-old marketing manager, often felt anxious and disorganized at home. Her apartment was filled with papers, clothes, and random items scattered everywhere, which made her feel overwhelmed. After reading about the connection between clutter and stress, Laura decided to declutter her living space. She started by organizing her bedroom and created a designated "calm zone" where she could unwind. Laura immediately noticed that she felt more relaxed in her new space, and her anxiety levels decreased as her environment became more orderly.

Practical Tip: Decluttering your space can have a calming effect on your mind and body. Start by organizing one room at a time, and create a clutter-free zone where you can relax and recharge.

8.2
Managing Digital Stress and Reducing Cortisol

In today's digital world, constant connectivity can be a major source of stress. The pressure to stay on top of emails, social media notifications, and work tasks can keep your brain in a state of hyperactivity, leading to elevated cortisol levels. Managing digital overload is an important step in lowering stress and creating a more balanced lifestyle.

The Effects of Screen Time on Cortisol

Excessive screen time—whether from work, social media, or entertainment—can lead to elevated cortisol levels. This is especially true when screen time extends into the evening, as the blue light emitted by phones, tablets, and computers disrupts the body's natural sleep-wake cycle.

Case Study: Tom's Digital Detox

Tom, a 45-year-old sales manager, spent most of his day in front of a computer for work and often unwound by scrolling through social media at night. He found it hard to disconnect, even after work hours, and his stress levels were constantly high. After experiencing symptoms of burnout, Tom decided to do a digital detox. He set boundaries around screen time, such as no phone use during meals and no screen time after 8 p.m. He also replaced his evening scrolling with reading a book or practicing meditation. These small changes helped reduce Tom's cortisol levels, improve his focus, and enhance his sleep quality.

Practical Tip: Set boundaries around screen time by designating specific times of the day to check emails or social media. Avoid using devices at least an hour before bed, and consider doing a "digital detox" once a week, where you disconnect from all screens for a day.

Managing Email and Work-Related Stress

For many people, work-related stress is a significant contributor to elevated cortisol. Constantly checking emails, meeting deadlines, and managing workloads can keep your cortisol levels elevated throughout the day. Learning to manage work stress effectively can help lower cortisol and improve your overall well-being.

Practical Tip: Set specific times during the day to check and respond to emails rather than constantly monitoring your inbox. This can help reduce feelings of overwhelm and give you more control over your work tasks. Additionally, practice setting boundaries between work and personal time, especially if you work from home.

Case Study: Jessica's Email Boundaries

Jessica, a 37-year-old project manager, found herself checking emails late into the evening and responding to work messages at all hours. This constant connection to work made it difficult for her to relax and led to burnout. After attending a stress management workshop, Jessica set clear boundaries around her work hours. She stopped checking emails after 6 p.m. and set up an automatic "out of office" message for weekends. These boundaries allowed Jessica to recharge outside of work, leading to lower cortisol levels and better work-life balance.

8.3
Creating a Cortisol-Friendly Home and Workspace

Your home and workspace can either contribute to your stress or provide a calming sanctuary that helps reduce cortisol levels. Making simple adjustments to your surroundings can create an environment that promotes relaxation and well-being.

Optimizing Your Home for Relaxation

Here are a few tips for creating a cortisol-friendly home environment:

- **Add plants**: Indoor plants can improve air quality and have a calming effect on the mind. Research shows that spending time in nature, or even just looking at greenery, can reduce stress and lower cortisol.

- **Incorporate soothing colors**: Soft, neutral colors like light blues, greens, and grays can create a more calming atmosphere and help reduce stress. Avoid overly bright or stimulating colors in areas where you want to relax.

- **Use calming scents**: Essential oils like lavender, chamomile, and eucalyptus have been shown to promote relaxation and reduce stress. Use a diffuser or light candles with calming scents in areas where you want to unwind.

Case Study: Amanda's Relaxing Home Environment

Amanda, a 30-year-old graphic designer, wanted to create a more peaceful home environment after realizing how stressed she felt at home. She added a few indoor plants, replaced her bright red living room walls with a soft blue color, and started diffusing lavender essential oil in the evenings. These small changes made her home feel more serene, and Amanda found it easier to unwind after work, lowering her cortisol levels in the process.

Optimizing Your Workspace for Focus and Stress Reduction

Your workspace is another area where you can make adjustments to reduce cortisol and improve focus. Whether you work from home or in an office, creating an organized, comfortable workspace can help reduce stress and improve productivity.

Practical Tips for a Cortisol-Friendly Workspace:

- **Declutter your desk**: A clean, organized desk can help reduce feelings of overwhelm and improve focus.

- **Add plants or calming decorations**: A small plant or personal mementos can add warmth to your workspace and make it feel more inviting.

- **Optimize ergonomics**: Ensure that your chair, desk, and computer setup are ergonomically friendly to prevent physical discomfort, which can contribute to stress.

Case Study: Jason's Workspace Transformation

Jason, a 40-year-old accountant, found his work environment to be chaotic and stressful. His desk was cluttered with papers, and he often experienced neck pain from sitting at his computer all day. After reading about the connection between workspace ergonomics and stress, Jason decided to make some changes. He decluttered his desk, added a few indoor plants, and adjusted his chair and monitor to reduce strain. These changes helped reduce his physical discomfort and made his work environment feel more organized and less stressful, leading to lower cortisol levels.

8.4
Time Management and Work-Life Balance

Finding balance between work and personal life is essential for managing stress and keeping cortisol levels in check. Poor time management and overworking can lead to chronic stress, while effective time management can help you feel more in control and reduce cortisol levels.

Setting Boundaries Between Work and Personal Time

Setting boundaries around work hours is critical for maintaining a healthy work-life balance. If you often find yourself working late or responding to emails after hours, you may need to establish clear boundaries to protect your personal time.

Case Study: Sophie's Work-Life Balance

Sophie, a 32-year-old lawyer, often found herself working late into the night and answering emails during weekends. This constant connection to work left her feeling stressed and burnt out. After discussing her workload with her boss, Sophie was able to set clearer boundaries, leaving work at a reasonable time and disconnecting from emails after 6 p.m. This shift allowed her to recharge during her personal time, significantly lowering her stress levels and improving her well-being.

8.5
Building Strong Relationships to Reduce Cortisol

Strong social connections and supportive relationships are powerful tools for managing stress and lowering cortisol levels. Research shows that individuals with close friendships and strong family bonds experience lower levels of cortisol during stressful situations.

The Role of Social Support in Stress Reduction

Spending time with loved ones, talking about your problems, and seeking support from others can significantly reduce stress and lower cortisol. On the other hand, loneliness and isolation can increase stress and elevate cortisol levels.

Case Study: Rachel's Support Network

Rachel, a 38-year-old nurse, often felt overwhelmed by the demands of her job. However, she found comfort in spending time with her close friends and family, who provided her with emotional support and understanding. By leaning on her support network, Rachel was able to cope with the challenges of her job and keep her stress levels in check.

8.6
Conclusion: Creating a Lifestyle That Supports Low Cortisol

Your environment, digital habits, and lifestyle choices all play a significant role in regulating cortisol levels. By making simple adjustments to your home, workspace, and daily habits, you can create a more calming and supportive environment that promotes relaxation and reduces stress.

Incorporating strategies such as managing digital overload, optimizing your living and working spaces, setting boundaries around work, and building strong relationships can all help reduce cortisol and improve your overall well-being.

In the next chapter, we'll explore how to create a sustainable, long-term plan for managing cortisol and maintaining a healthy, low-stress lifestyle.

Chapter 9:
Creating a Sustainable Low-Cortisol Lifestyle

Cortisol management is not a one-time effort but a continuous practice that requires attention to both your mental and physical well-being. Creating a sustainable, low-stress lifestyle involves integrating the tools and techniques we've covered in the previous chapters into your daily routine. In this chapter, we'll explore how to make these practices a lasting part of your life, ensuring that you maintain balanced cortisol levels and enjoy better long-term health.

9.1
Building Long-Term Habits for Stress Reduction

The key to managing cortisol over the long term is consistency. Many people experience short-term success with stress reduction techniques but struggle to maintain these habits in the face of daily challenges. The goal is to create lasting routines that become second nature, helping you manage stress and keep cortisol levels in check no matter what life throws your way.

Start Small and Build Gradually

One of the most effective ways to create lasting change is to start small. Instead of trying to overhaul your entire lifestyle at once, begin by incorporating one or two simple stress-reduction techniques into your daily routine. Over time, these small changes will build up, creating a sustainable foundation for cortisol management.

Case Study: Lisa's Gradual Lifestyle Shift

Lisa, a 34-year-old marketing executive, had always struggled with stress management. She tried adopting multiple techniques at once—meditation, yoga, and a new diet—but found it overwhelming and quickly gave up. After reflecting on her experience, Lisa decided to take a different approach. She started with a 5-minute meditation practice each morning. Once that became a habit, she added a weekly yoga class, and later, began making small changes to her diet. By building gradually, Lisa was able to maintain these habits long-term and saw a noticeable improvement in her stress levels and overall well-being.

Practical Tip: Start with just one or two techniques—such as mindfulness meditation or improving your sleep habits—and focus on consistency. Once these practices become routine, you can gradually add more stress-reduction strategies to your life.

9.2
Prioritizing Self-Care and Mental Health

Self-care is often the first thing to be sacrificed when life gets busy, but it is essential for managing stress and maintaining balanced cortisol levels. Prioritizing mental and emotional well-being is crucial for long-term cortisol management and overall health.

The Role of Self-Care in Cortisol Regulation

Taking time to care for your mental and emotional health is not a luxury but a necessity. Regular self-care practices can help reduce cortisol levels by providing time for relaxation, reflection, and mental rejuvenation.

Case Study: Sarah's Self-Care Routine

Sarah, a 40-year-old teacher, often felt overwhelmed by her responsibilities at work and at home. She rarely took time for herself, which led to feelings of burnout and elevated cortisol levels. After attending a wellness retreat, Sarah decided to create a self-care routine. She began setting aside 30 minutes each evening to relax, whether through reading, taking a bath, or practicing yoga. These small acts of self-care helped her feel more balanced, and her stress levels significantly decreased over time.

Practical Tip: Incorporate daily or weekly self-care activities that help you relax and recharge. This could be as simple as taking a walk in nature, practicing meditation, or spending time with loved ones.

9.3
Time Management for Stress-Free Living

Time management is another key factor in reducing stress and keeping cortisol levels in check. Poor time management often leads to feelings of overwhelm, rushing to meet deadlines, and multitasking, all of which can increase cortisol. By managing your time effectively, you can reduce these stressors and create more balance in your life.

Practical Time Management Strategies

Here are a few time management strategies that can help reduce stress and lower cortisol:

- **Prioritize tasks**: Focus on the most important tasks first, and don't be afraid to delegate or say no to less important ones.

- **Break tasks into smaller steps**: Large tasks can feel overwhelming, leading to stress. Break them down into smaller, manageable steps, and tackle one step at a time.

- **Set time limits**: Set a specific amount of time for each task, and stick to it. This helps prevent procrastination and keeps you on track.

- **Create a daily schedule**: Plan your day in advance, allocating time for work, relaxation, and self-care. Having a schedule can help reduce uncertainty and create a sense of control.

Case Study: Mike's Time Management Success

Mike, a 38-year-old entrepreneur, often felt overwhelmed by the demands of running his own business. He worked long hours, often late into the night, and his cortisol levels were constantly elevated. After consulting with a time management coach, Mike learned to prioritize his tasks and create a structured daily schedule that included dedicated time for work, exercise, and relaxation. By managing his time more effectively, Mike was able to reduce his stress and maintain better work-life balance.

9.4
Building Emotional Resilience and Coping Skills

Emotional resilience—the ability to adapt to and recover from stress—is essential for managing cortisol levels in the long term. Developing healthy coping mechanisms and learning to manage emotions effectively can prevent cortisol spikes during challenging situations.

The Importance of Emotional Resilience

Emotional resilience doesn't mean avoiding stress altogether but learning how to navigate stressful situations without becoming overwhelmed. By building emotional resilience, you can prevent cortisol from spiking unnecessarily and manage stress in a healthier way.

Case Study: Rachel's Resilience Journey

Rachel, a 45-year-old nurse, faced constant stress at work and often found herself feeling emotionally drained by the end of each day. After attending a workshop on emotional resilience, Rachel learned new coping strategies, such as reframing negative thoughts, practicing gratitude, and seeking support from friends and colleagues. Over time, Rachel became more resilient in handling stressful situations at work, and her cortisol levels stabilized as a result.

Practical Strategies for Building Emotional Resilience

Here are a few techniques that can help build emotional resilience:

- **Reframe negative thoughts**: When faced with a stressful situation, try to shift your perspective. Instead of focusing on the worst-case scenario, ask yourself, "What's the best possible outcome?"

- **Practice gratitude**: Focusing on the positive aspects of your life can help shift your mindset and reduce stress. Keep a gratitude journal where you write down three things you're grateful for each day.

- **Develop a support network**: Surround yourself with supportive friends, family, or colleagues who can offer encouragement and help during stressful times.

- **Practice acceptance**: Accept that stress is a part of life, and focus on how you can respond to it in a healthy way rather than trying to eliminate it completely.

9.5
Overcoming Setbacks: Staying Consistent with Cortisol Management

It's natural to experience setbacks along the way, especially when life gets busy or unexpected challenges arise. The key to long-term cortisol management is learning to stay consistent with your stress-reduction practices, even when things don't go as planned.

How to Handle Setbacks and Stay on Track

When you encounter setbacks—such as falling behind on self-care, skipping workouts, or experiencing a stressful event—it's important not to give up on your progress. Instead, approach setbacks with self-compassion and focus on getting back on track.

Case Study: John's Setback and Recovery

John, a 42-year-old architect, had been managing his stress well for months, using meditation and regular exercise to keep his cortisol levels in check. However, when his company faced an unexpected project deadline, John found himself working long hours and skipping his usual stress-relief practices. His cortisol levels spiked, and he felt more stressed than ever. After reflecting on the situation, John realized that setbacks were a normal part of life. He refocused on his self-care routine, gradually reintroducing meditation and exercise into his daily schedule. Over time, John was able to regain control of his stress and maintain balance.

Practical Tip: When you experience a setback, don't be too hard on yourself. Reflect on what caused the setback and make a plan to reintroduce your stress-reduction practices. Focus on consistency rather than perfection.

9.6
Creating a Personalized Low-Cortisol Lifestyle Plan

Now that we've covered a range of techniques for managing stress and lowering cortisol, it's time to create a personalized plan that works for you. Your low-cortisol lifestyle plan should include a combination of the techniques and practices that resonate with you the most.

Step-by-Step Guide to Creating Your Plan

1. **Identify your main stressors**: Make a list of the key factors in your life that contribute to stress and elevated cortisol levels. This could include work-related stress, lack of sleep, poor time management, or relationship issues.

2. **Choose your stress-reduction techniques**: Select the techniques that work best for you from the chapters we've covered. This might include mindfulness meditation, yoga, time management strategies, or improving your sleep habits.

3. **Set specific goals**: Define clear, actionable goals for each area of your life. For example, your goal might be to meditate for 10 minutes each morning, exercise three times a week, or limit screen time in the evenings.

4. **Create a daily or weekly routine**: Plan when and how you will incorporate these stress-reduction techniques into your daily or weekly schedule. The key is to make them a regular part of your routine, rather than an occasional practice.

5. **Track your progress**: Keep track of how you're feeling over time. You might want to journal about your stress levels, energy, and mood each day. Reflect on what's working and make adjustments as needed.

6. **Be flexible**: Life will inevitably throw challenges your way, so be flexible with your plan. If something isn't working, adjust it to fit your current circumstances. The goal is to create a sustainable routine that supports your long-term health and well-being.

9.7 Conclusion: Maintaining a Balanced Lifestyle for Long-Term Health

Creating a sustainable, low-cortisol lifestyle is about more than just reducing stress in the short term—it's about building lasting habits that support your overall health and well-being. By incorporating stress-reduction techniques, prioritizing self-care, and managing your time effectively, you can maintain balanced cortisol levels and enjoy better physical and mental health over the long term.

Remember, it's not about achieving perfection but about making consistent, small changes that lead to lasting results. By staying committed to your low-cortisol lifestyle plan, you can experience lower stress, better energy, and improved well-being for years to come.

Conclusion: Your Cortisol Journey

Throughout this book, we have explored the powerful impact cortisol has on your body and mind. While cortisol is an essential hormone that plays a key role in managing stress and supporting vital functions, it can cause significant harm when out of balance. Chronic stress and elevated cortisol levels can lead to a host of health problems, from weight gain and fatigue to cardiovascular disease and cognitive decline.

However, by understanding how cortisol works and applying practical strategies to manage it, you can take control of your stress, improve your health, and enhance your overall quality of life. The tools and techniques presented in this book—ranging from nutrition and exercise to mindfulness, sleep, and environmental adjustments—are designed to help you lower cortisol and manage stress more effectively.

Key Takeaways: What You've Learned

Let's take a moment to recap the key lessons from each chapter:

- **Understanding Cortisol**: You learned about the role of cortisol as a stress hormone and its importance in regulating metabolism, immune function, and energy levels. We also explored how chronic stress disrupts the delicate balance of cortisol in the body, leading to long-term health problems.

- **What Increases Cortisol**: Physical stressors such as injury, illness, and intense exercise, as well as psychological stressors like anxiety and trauma, can all trigger cortisol spikes. Lifestyle factors such as poor sleep, an unhealthy diet, and excessive screen time can further contribute to elevated cortisol.

- **The Impact of Cortisol on Your Body and Mind**: Prolonged elevated cortisol levels can weaken the immune system, cause weight gain (especially around the abdomen), and lead to cognitive decline. Mental health is also affected, with chronic stress leading to anxiety, depression, and mood swings.

- **Nutrition and Cortisol**: What you eat can either raise or lower cortisol. Refined sugars, processed foods, and caffeine tend to increase cortisol, while complex carbohydrates, healthy fats, leafy greens, and Omega-3s can help reduce it. Supplements like ashwagandha and magnesium can also support cortisol balance.

- **Exercise and Cortisol**: Physical activity is a powerful tool for managing stress, but it's important to find the right balance between high-intensity and low-intensity workouts. While intense exercise can cause temporary cortisol spikes, incorporating rest days and low-intensity activities like yoga can help keep cortisol levels in check.

- **The Importance of Sleep**: Sleep is one of the most effective ways to regulate cortisol. By maintaining a consistent sleep schedule, optimizing your sleep environment, and practicing good sleep hygiene, you can improve the quality of your rest and lower cortisol.

- **Stress Management Techniques**: Mindfulness, meditation, yoga, breathing exercises, and cognitive-behavioral techniques are all powerful tools for reducing cortisol and managing stress. Practicing gratitude and positive thinking can further support a low-stress lifestyle.

- **Environmental and Lifestyle Adjustments**: Your environment and daily habits can significantly impact cortisol levels. By managing digital stress, creating a relaxing home and workspace, and building strong relationships, you can reduce stress and create a more supportive environment for your health.

- **Creating a Sustainable Low-Cortisol Lifestyle**: Building long-term habits, prioritizing self-care, and managing your time effectively are all crucial for maintaining balanced cortisol

About the Author

Dr. Alexander Montrose is a renowned neuroscientist and expert in the fields of endocrinology and integrative health, with over 20 years of experience helping patients manage stress, balance hormones, and improve their overall well-being. He earned his medical degree from the University of Zurich and has since dedicated his career to understanding how hormones like cortisol impact physical and mental health.

Dr. Montrose has conducted and participated in numerous studies on the physiological effects of chronic stress, hormone regulation, and metabolic health. His research has been published in several respected journals, and he frequently lectures at medical conferences around the world. Some of his key areas of study include:

- **The impact of cortisol on metabolic syndrome:** Dr. Montrose's research has contributed to understanding how prolonged cortisol elevation can lead to conditions like insulin resistance, weight gain, and Type 2 diabetes. His work builds on foundational studies in the field, such as the research by Rosmond et al. on "Cortisol and Metabolic Syndrome."

- **Stress management and mental health:** Dr. Montrose has been actively involved in exploring how stress-reduction techniques, including mindfulness and cognitive-behavioral therapy (CBT), can lower cortisol levels and improve mood. His studies align with the work of Davidson et al., which demonstrated the benefits of mindfulness-based approaches for managing stress and anxiety.

- **The role of nutrition and exercise in hormone balance:** Understanding the relationship between diet, physical activity, and hormone regulation is a major focus of Dr. Montrose's practice. He has been a part of collaborative studies that examine how balanced nutrition and regular exercise can support healthy cortisol levels, consistent with findings in research by Hill et al. on "Diet and Exercise Impact on Hormonal Balance."

As a dedicated advocate for patient education, Dr. Montrose believes that knowledge is power. In *Understanding Cortisol*, he combines the latest scientific insights with practical advice, empowering readers to take control of their health and manage stress effectively.